Totally Gross

TOtally Gross

by Mary Packard

and the Editors of Ripley Entertainment Inc.

illustrations by Leanne Franson

SCHOLASTIC INC.

New York   Toronto   London   Auckland   Sydney
Mexico City   New Delhi   Hong Kong   Buenos Aires

Developed by Nancy Hall, Inc.
Designed by R studio T
Cover design by Atif Toor
Photo research by Laura Miller

ISBN 0-439-63367-2

Printed in the U.S.A.
First printing, February 2004

Contents

Totally Gross

Introduction

The Yuck Factor

Now and then we all have an experience that is totally gross. The yuck factor is a part of life that everyone can identify with. No one likes to step in a pile of dog poop or bite into a wormy apple. But such revolting scenes in books and movies never fail to make us laugh. The truth is it's great fun to experience

disgusting stuff—especially when it's happening to someone else. No one had a better understanding of just how entertaining the yuck factor can be than Robert Ripley, creator of Believe It or Not!

Robert Ripley was the first cartoonist to become a millionaire. One of the most interesting personalities of the 20th century, he traveled the globe in search of the oddest, most bizarre, and extraordinary people, places, and things to feature in his drawings. His cartoons were such a big hit with the public that by 1922, his readership had swelled to 80 million. While doing research for his column, nothing delighted Robert Ripley more than to stumble across gross things that made other people shudder—be it ground-up mummy skin as a cure for disease or a recipe for maggot cheese.

In *Totally Gross,* you'll read about lots of nasty things, such as the millions of microscopic bugs you share your bed with, not to mention all the ones inside your mouth. There are also stories about nasty events, such as insect infestations and really foul weather, that are guaranteed to make you cringe. The pages of *Totally Gross* are filled with—well,

totally gross stories and facts. In each chapter, you can also test your gross-o-meter by taking the Yuck! quizzes and solving the Brain Buster. Then you can try the special Pop Quiz at the end of the book and use the scorecard to find out your Ripley's Rank.

So get ready to gross out your friends with some of the foulest facts you've ever heard. But beware. Don't even think about reading this book just before dinnertime. *Totally Gross* is definitely not a book for the squeamish!

Believe It!®

After you read this chapter, you'll never complain about eating your veggies again!

Bring on the Grub! Moth larvae, anyone? The witchetty grub, the larva of the ghost moth, which is found in the roots of the witchetty bush, is a favorite treat in Australia. It's lightly crunchy when baked, soft and buttery when eaten raw, and even tastier when toasted on a stick.

Yuck!

A company in the United States makes lollipops embedded with . . .

a. seaweed.
b. fish eggs.
c. worms.
d. mud.

Buried Treasure:

Mix up some fish heads, fins, tails, and guts in a pot and bury them in the ground for a few months. Once they've decayed, just dig them up and they're ready to serve. The Inuit of Alaska like this thick paste as a spread to go with some of their other favorite foods.

Chew Your Food . . . unless you can get an animal to do it for you, that is. After hunting, the Inuit of Alaska used to cut open an animal's stomach to get at the prize inside—the partly digested green vegetables and grasses that the animal ate for lunch. At the time, these secondhand veggies were considered a delicacy.

Creepy-Crawly Diet: Many of the more than 1,450 species of edible insects not only taste good but also are a great source of protein, vitamins, and minerals. But don't eat one unless you know what it is—it could be poisonous.

Yuck!

In New Guinea, people can snack on the parts of their necklaces made out of . . .

a. cicada wings.
b. sago maggots.
c. dried Venus's-flytraps.
d. oysters.

Bug Buffet: In case you'd like to try your hand at creating a bug dinner party of your own, there are several books that can help you with the menu. A few of them are *Entertaining with Insects* by Ronald L. Taylor, *Eat-a-Bug Cookbook* by David George Gordon, and *Creepy Crawly Cuisine* by Julieta Ramos-Elorduy.

Essence of Beaver:

Raspberry is used to flavor all sorts of beverages and desserts. It's often combined with castoreum, which tends to enhance the flavor of raspberry and make it stand out among other ingredients. What exactly is castoreum? It's a substance found in the anal musk glands of beavers. Raspberry sherbet, anyone?

Snakes Alive! In Hong Kong, snakes are the chief ingredient in both a popular broth and in a potent wine.

Mind Your Own Beeswax: In many parts of the world, people eat something called bee brood, a mix of bee larvae and pupae. This tasty treat can be eaten in the comb taken straight from the hive or cooked in a number of ways, including fried and baked. Packed with vitamins and minerals, bee brood not only tastes good (so we're told) but also is very nutritious.

Crunch and Munch! Termites cooked in oil and salt are a delicacy among the Bantu tribe in South Africa.

Pigging Out: In Europe and in the southern United States Cajun country, the blood of freshly slaughtered pigs is cooked and made into blood sausage, which is sometimes called blood pudding or black sausage. In Germany, people even eat pig's blood plain in a dish called fried blood. Of course, if you want something a little heartier, you can always try *schlachtplatte,* which literally means "slaughter dish," a stew made with all the body parts of a pig.

Bloodthirsty: Ireland has its own version of blood pudding. First cows are bled, then the blood is boiled with milk, butter, and spices. When the mixture cools, it turns to a kind of gelatin. Cut it into squares and it's ready to eat.

Yuck!

In Myanmar (formerly Burma), a favorite recipe features a savory pork filling stuffed into . . .

a. snail shells.
b. snake skins.
c. alligator eggs.
d. crickets.

Hamming It Up: Ham is made from the thighs of pigs. And guess what! Ham from the left rear leg is more tender than ham from the right rear leg because pigs build up muscles in their right leg—the one they use to scratch themselves.

Fuzzy Food: In Africa, the caterpillar of the mopane emperor moth is a favorite delicacy. It can be stewed, fried, or, for those who can't wait, eaten fresh from the tree.

Foul Feast: A typical banquet in ancient Rome consisted of pike liver, pheasant brain, lamprey eggs, peacock brain, and the tongue of a flamingo.

Spitting It Up:

Not all nests are for birds. In China, people use them to make bird's-nest soup. Only the nests made from one kind of bird will do, however—the nests made by swiftlets. Here's how these sparrow-sized birds

do it. The male birds regurgitate long, thin strands of saliva, which are shaped into cuplike nests. The sticky saliva not only holds the nests together but also acts as a cement to make them stick to the walls of the caves where the birds live. The most prized nest is that of the edible-nest swiftlet. That's because it's pure saliva without anything mixed in. In some restaurants, a bowl of bird's-nest soup can cost more than $50.

Yuck!

To find out if brightly colored wildlife tastes more disgusting than the drab variety of the same species, a group of college students went to Costa Rica to compare the taste of various types of uncooked . . .

a. tadpoles.
b. butterflies.
c. caterpillars.
d. crickets.

Creepy Cuisine:

Vegetable caterpillar is another fine food that is sold in China. It is made when a fungus has eaten the insides of a caterpillar. It's sold encased in a caterpillar skin.

Finger Food: In England, a specialty of many street vendors is jellied eel. Cut into finger-length pieces, they are just the right size for an instant snack. D-eel-icious!

Baa! Grind up the heart, lungs, and liver of a sheep. Mix it with oatmeal and fat, then stuff it all into the sheep's stomach. Tie it off so that the mixture doesn't leak, then drop the stomach into a pot of boiling water. Simmer, cool, and you have a pudding called haggis, a traditional Scottish dish that is served on holidays. Yum!

Over the Top:

Mushrooms add great flavor to many wonderful dishes. But did you know that they are grown with poop? Spores, which are the reproductive part of the mushroom, are

sprinkled on fresh manure and covered with soil. Before long, tiny mushrooms spring up and grow a little bigger every day. Mushroom pizza, anyone?

Yuck!

Indonesian luak coffee is the most expensive coffee in the world. It is called luak coffee after a type of bobcat because . . .

a. the bean is the same color as the luak.
b. luaks like to spray the coffee plants, greatly adding to the flavor of the beans.
c. the beans taste better after they've been digested by a luak and separated from its poop.
d. luaks make their nests in coffee trees, making the beans extremely difficult and expensive to harvest.

Die-hard Habit:

In many parts of the world, human flesh was once considered a normal part of the diet. In Sumatra, Indonesia, and parts of western Africa, human meat was even sold in local markets. On the island of Fiji, human flesh was called "long pig." Today, however, eating human flesh is against the law in most parts of the world.

Crispy Critters: How would you like a bag of grasshoppers fried in garlic and lemon to go? When people in Oaxaca, Mexico, are in the mood for a flavorful snack, that's just what they order.

Beetle Juice: In ancient Rome, chefs liked to prepare the larvae of the stag beetle in a variety of ways. But before whipping up their gourmet creations, they fed the larvae a diet of flour and wine. Only then were they fat and juicy enough to serve to their guests.

Waste Not, Want Not: Gelatin is made from animal skins, hooves, and skeletons. It's used as a thickener for many types of foods, such as ice cream and cereal.

Fish Balls: Gefilte fish is a tasty Yiddish dish that consists of balls of ground fish mixed with onions and poached in a broth. Some people serve it in a jellied broth that has been made out of fish bones. The Yiddish name for the jellied stuff is *yuk*—which exactly describes how some people feel about eating it!

> ## Yuck!
>
> In Malaya, fried grubs are a popular treat. The grubs are found by sifting through . . .
>
> **a.** seaweed.
> **b.** cattle dung.
> **c.** horse manure.
> **d.** garbage.

Totally Stuffed! A traditional Bedouin wedding feast includes an egg-filled fish placed inside a chicken, which in turn is put inside a whole sheep. Then the whole shebang is roasted inside a camel.

Heads Up: Don't be fooled. Headcheese is really not a cheese at all. It is a jellied lunch meat made from the boiled heads of animals. Popular in Europe, it's served chilled and is often the main ingredient in a sandwich.

Yuck!

Considered a delicacy in China, sea cucumbers are actually . . .

a. jellyfish.
b. sea slugs.
c. sea snakes.
d. blowfish.

On the Fly: A special kind of spread is made in Sardinia, Italy. To make it, you cover a wedge of cheese with cheesecloth and leave it outside for the flies. After they have laid their eggs on it and the maggots have hatched, the cheese is ready to spread on bread—maggots and all. It's called maggot cheese. Eat up.

Sweet Treats: Some honey-pot ants in a colony serve as storage ants. They are fed so much honey that they swell up to twice their normal size. The skin over their abdomens is stretched so thin, you can see right through them. In fact, they sometimes swell up so  much that they pop! People in Italy and Australia can't get enough of these sweet and crunchy treats.

Gag-alicious! Here's a little-known fact: The United States Food and Drug Administration, better known as the FDA—the agency charged with ensuring that foods are safe, wholesome, sanitary, and properly labeled—permits a limited number of small bug parts to be included in processed food. That's because it's impossible to grow crops free of all insects without using dangerous amounts of pesticides. A jar of peanut butter may include more than 100 itsy-bitsy bug parts, while canned tomatoes might contain one maggot and as many as nine fly eggs. Just think of it this way: You're getting a little extra protein in your food!

Apple Polisher: Would you choose a shiny apple or a dull one? Most of us would choose the shiny apple. But we might make a different choice if we knew how the shiny apple got that way. Shellac made from insect poop is used to make all kinds of food shiny—from apples to peanut butter. Why? Because shiny food looks more appetizing.

There's a Fly in My Soup! In the early 1990s, a popular restaurant in Washington, D.C., was called The Insect Club. A typical meal consisted of fried mealworms for an appetizer, roasted Australian grubs (juicy little sausages with a mouth on one end) and worm balls in spicy tomato sauce as the entrée, and to top it all off, cricket brittle for dessert. Chef Marc Nevin said that he went through 20,000 mealworms and 8,000 crickets every two weeks.

Yuck!

The main ingredient in a type of pie made in Japan is . . .

a. mosquitoes.
b. ants.
c. grasshoppers.
d. worms.

Hairy Little Secret: If you find 1-cysteine listed among the ingredients in your favorite foods, you might be surprised to know where it comes from. 1-cysteine is an amino acid that is extracted from human hair. It is used to make dough stretchy in pizza, cookies, doughnuts, and many of the other pastry goodies we all love to eat.

Yuck!

Pink lemonade was invented in 1857 when circus performer Pete Conklin unwittingly made lemonade using a bucket of water that . . .

a. another performer had soaked his red tights in.
b. he'd contaminated with blood from a cut on his finger.
c. had red paint in it.
d. contained a rusty nail.

Brain Buster

Time to get down and dirty and test your ability to tell what's *truly* gross from something that's gross— but completely *un*true!

Robert Ripley dedicated his life to seeking out the bizarre and unusual. But every unbelievable thing he recorded was known to be true. In the Brain Buster at the end of every chapter, you'll play Ripley's role—trying to verify the fantastic facts presented. Each Ripley's Brain Buster contains a group of four shocking statements. But of these so-called "facts," **one** is **fiction**. Will you **Believe It!** or **Not!**?

Wait—there's more! Following the Brain Busters are special bonus questions where you can earn extra points! Keep score by flipping to the end of the book for the answer key and a scorecard.

Sometimes the truth can be really hard to swallow. Can you tell the difference between the treats you might find on a real menu and the one that's completely imaginary?

a. *Hachi-no-ko*, boiled wasp larvae, and *sangi*, fried silk moth pupae, are popular dishes in Tokyo.
          Believe It!   **Not!**

21

b. Steak tartare dates back to Medieval Russia but is now enjoyed in many countries. What is it? Ground raw beef mixed with spices and served with a raw egg on top.

Believe It!   **Not!**

c. In China, a dish called drunken shrimp is a specialty of many eateries. The live shrimp are served swimming in a bowl of rice wine, and patrons bite off the heads of the shrimp before eating the bodies.

Believe It!   **Not!**

d. Tibetan tiger tonsils are a rare delicacy in the Himalayas, especially when they're eaten with boiled yak tongue.

Believe It!   **Not!**

• •

BONUS QUESTION

A standout item on a Newfoundland menu is . . .

a. seal flipper pie.

b. jellyfish cobbler.

c. cow cartilage salad.

d. oyster pudding.

Have you ever stopped to think about what goes down your throat besides food? Or that millions of tiny creatures call your body home? In this chapter, you'll find out more than you ever wanted to know!

Yuck!

About every three minutes, children touch their mouths with their hands and end up swallowing . . .

a. enough dirt each day to cover seven floor tiles.
b. an average of one bug every day.
c. enough dust to cover a twin-sized bed.
d. enough paste in one year to fill a cookie jar.

Say It Snot True:
Mucus is made in the lining of the nose. When you have a cold, your nose gets runny because your body is trying to flush out those cold germs. Did you know that even when you're not sick, you swallow about a quart of snot every single day?

Achoo! Run for cover! Here's an amazingly gross though little-known fact: The drops of moisture in a sneeze can travel up to 150 feet per second. That's 102 miles per hour!

Really Flaky: Did you know that you shed your skin? Every day, you lose about ten billion flakes of dead skin. If you saved all those flakes for your entire life, they would fill a 5-pound bag.

Got a Bug?

Eye Strain: Hundreds of microscopic creatures called follicle mites are tucked into the roots of your eyelashes.

What a Louse! The bad news is head lice are parasites that thrive on sucking the blood from your scalp. The good news is they die just as soon as they are removed.

Room Spray: With each flush of the toilet, hundreds of thousands of microscopic water droplets hit the air—each and every one of them is filled with intestinal bacteria.

What's for

Crispy Critters: In Oaxaca, Mexico, grasshoppers are sold in outdoor markets. Then they're boiled with salt, garlic, lime juice, and spices for a flavorful snack.

Creepy-Crawly Diet: You may be squeamish about eating bugs, but many of them actually taste good. They are also a great source of proteins, vitamins, and minerals. There are more than 1,450 species of edible insects, but be careful. Don't eat a bug unless you know what it is. Many are poisonous.

Lunch?

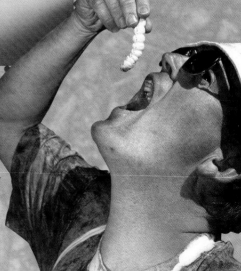

A Bellyful: The storage ants in a honey-pot ant colony are fed so much honey, their abdomen sometimes pops! These roly-poly little insects serve as crunchy treats in Italy and Australia.

Pass the Spider: Instead of hamburgers, the Piaroa Indians of Venezuela roast 11-inch tarantulas over the fire.

Good Grub: The witchetty grub, a moth larva, is a favorite treat in Australia.

Gross Practices

What a Gas! Joseph Pujol, a French entertainer in the late 1800s, did imitations of cannon fire, machine guns, musical scores, and thunder—all by passing gas!

Cheek-kabob: Participants in the Vegetarian Festival in Thailand skewer themselves instead of the food, puncturing their cheeks with knives, skewers, and other implements. Ouch!

Bloodsuckers: The practice of curing illness by using leeches to drain excess blood was discredited 100 years ago. Now the little bloodsuckers are back. Plastic surgeons have found that they're the most effective means of draining excess blood from reattached limbs or transplanted skin.

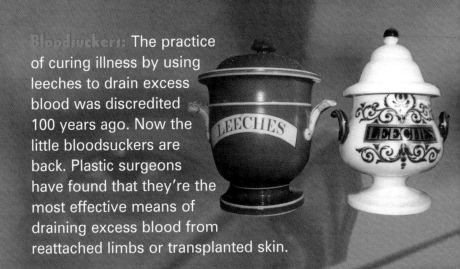

Pigging Out: In Philadelphia, pigs get the Thanksgiving leftovers after the farmers comb through garbage, collecting thousands of tons of food!

Fat Attack! Don "Moses" Lerman gobbled up seven quarter-pound salted butter sticks in five minutes in a competitive eating contest.

HOW

Bless You! Did you know that the drops of moisture in a sneeze can travel more than 100 miles per hour?

The Inside Story: Grossology is a traveling interactive exhibit where kids can learn about the human body. Young visitors get to play "gas attack" pinball, climb a wart- and pimple-covered wall, and pass through a 30-foot-long, 3-D model of the digestive system.

Nasty!

Novelty Nuggets: In Alaska, moose droppings are shellacked and turned into novelty gifts, such as pencil toppers, swizzle sticks, key chains, and flowering moose nuggets.

Not So Shipshape: In 1976, people sailing in the Olympic Games were pelted by live maggots that fell from the sky during a storm!

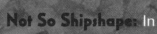

CRICKETS ON HIGHWAY
SLICK ROAD

Slimed! In 2003, thousands of Mormon crickets invaded Nevada, making the roads so slick that overhead signs were used to warn motorists.

Mad Medicine

Couldn't Stomach It: In 1822, Alexis St. Martin was shot in the stomach. His wound left a gaping hole in his side, so his doctor tied bits of food onto strings, dropped them inside, and later pulled them out to learn how the stomach digests food.

Shock Treatment: Torpedo rays were used to deliver shocks that were thought to cure headaches and other pain in ancient Rome.

Mummy Magic: In Europe during the 12th century, ancient Egyptian mummy skin with the wrappings still sticking to it was boiled and ground up for use as a medicine.

Wash It Out with Soap! The human mouth is a pretty disgusting place. Inside it live more germs than in any other part of the body. In fact, 100 million tiny organisms camp out in your mouth, eating the leftovers they find there,

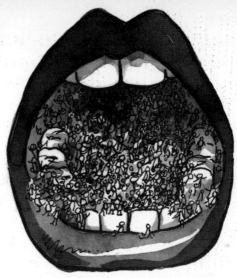

pooping, mating, and having babies—all in an average day. That's more than all the people in California, New York, Texas, Florida, Pennsylvania, and Michigan put together!

Acid Test: After you eat, the food gets broken up in your stomach so that the nutrients can be absorbed by your body. Inside your stomach are 35 million tiny vats that make acid so strong it can dissolve stainless steel!

Yuck!

In the 1700s, an Italian scientist named Lazzaro Spallanzani performed many revolting experiments on vomit. One of his conclusions was that . . .

a. a bucket of vomit will keep bears away.
b. food bits in vomit continue to be digested outside the body.
c. butterfly vomit smells like flowers.
d. some people vomit hair balls just like cats do.

Sleep Tight: You're not the only one who enjoys that comfy mattress and fluffy pillow you sleep on. Whether you know it or not, you have plenty of company. Millions of microscopic organisms called dust mites share your bed each night!

Eye Strain: Having trouble keeping your eyes open? That could be because your eyelids are heavy with hundreds of microscopic creatures called follicle mites, which live at the roots of your eyelashes!

Lousy Research:

In the past, scientists who created lice shampoos found it hard to study head lice. That's because the creatures die as soon as they're plucked from heads. Lice are parasites that need the blood of other species to survive. So researchers came up with the perfect solution—scalp in a test tube. The lice live on membranes and hair suspended in blood. This environment is perfect for keeping the pests alive just long enough to find out the best way to kill them!

Yuck!

To clear people out of public places without harming them, United States researchers are developing . . .

a. Robo Rooter, a robot with an electrical cattle prodder.
b. an odor bomb that smells like vomit and human wastes.
c. a machine that emits noise so loud that it is unbearable to the human ear.
d. Jet Slime, a machine that floods large areas with worms.

Room Spray: The next time you brush your teeth, think about this: Each flush of the toilet sends hundreds of thousands of microscopic water droplets chock-full of intestinal bacteria floating around the bathroom. Better keep that toothbrush tucked safely in a drawer!

Making a Stink:

Nine-year-old Danny Denault of New Milford, Connecticut, was the proud winner of a $500 prize in the Odor-Eaters Rotten Sneaker Contest. Asked the secret of his success, Danny had a quick response. "Cow pies," he replied. "They're just hard to avoid. They're everywhere."

Flea-for-All:

The flea that causes the most horrible itch is the chigger. That's because it doesn't stay on the surface of your skin. Instead, it burrows underneath the skin, where it lays its eggs—and after they hatch, the baby chiggers have to eat their way out. Ouch!

Yuck!

A cockroach can live without its head for . . .

a. one hour.
b. a few minutes.
c. nine days.
d. one day.

The Up-chuck Diet:

Those adorable little birds singing outside your window have a very unique way of feeding their young. First, they fill up on worms and other creepy-crawly

creatures. Then, after their meal has been well digested, they throw it up into their babies' open beaks. Instant baby food!

What a Gas! Joseph

Pujol, France's highest-paid entertainer in the late 1800s, made his fans laugh so hard that many of them passed out. Known as *Le Pétomane* (roughly translated as "fartiste"), he did imitations of cannon fire, machine guns, musical scores, and thunder—all by passing gas!

Sweating It Out:

To a person with a sensitive nose, the way someone smells can be a good indication of what he or she is feeling. Denise Chen, who is a researcher at the Monell Chemical Senses Center, did an experiment to find out if people could sniff out each other's moods. She provided 25 men and women with underarm pads, then showed them scenes from the movies *Indiana Jones* and *Ace Ventura*. Afterward, she took the pads and shuffled them. Then she passed them around, asking everyone to sniff the pads and say whether the wearer had been watching the funny movie or the scary one. About 75 percent of the time, the women were right about the men's pads. They were right about the women's pads about 50 percent of the time. How did the men do? Let's just say that when it came to sniffing out people's moods, they were totally clueless.

Yuck!

In 1930, Howard Frick of the University of Illinois blew so hard on his trumpet that he . . .

a. blew his brains out.
b. popped his eyes out of his head.
c. blew his tonsils out.
d. threw up on his audience.

Gag me! Body odor is caused when fats and proteins produced by our glands mix with bacteria that like to eat them. The bacteria excrete an acid that quickly evaporates, sending lots of smelly molecules into the air. If someone is around to receive them, they usually find their way up a pair of nostrils. Once inside the nose, the molecules dissolve in a special patch of mucus. This area is home to about 30 million nerve cells. The smelly molecules bind with receptors on the nerve cells that send a message to the brain that makes us say, "Pee-ew!"

Good Pickin's: Each year at Thanksgiving time, pig farmers in Philadelphia, Pennsylvania, collect some 24,000 tons of leftover food from curbside trash cans to feed to their pigs.

Eggs-tremely Disgusting:

Have you ever watched a fly land on your food for a second or two and then fly away? Did you continue eating? Next time, you might want to eat something else. Houseflies like nothing better than to lay their eggs on piles of poop or mounds of garbage. When they land on your food, their feet are probably still covered with you know what!

Really Trashy!

Have you ever thought about how much garbage the millions of people in a big city can generate? Unless you're a rat, it's not a pretty image. Just one day's garbage from New York City could easily fill the Empire State Building.

Testing the Waters: While British novelist Arnold Bennett (1867–1931) was visiting Paris, he drank a glass of tap water to prove that it was safe to drink—and died of typhoid fever shortly afterward.

Doot-ty Calls:

Participants at the annual Moose Dropping Festival in Talkeetna, Alaska, watch as a hot air balloon dumps 1,000 numbered pieces of moose droppings. The person who has the number of the piece that lands closest to an X etched on the ground wins $1,000.

Yuck!

When it's attacked, the sea cucumber defends itself by . . .

a. vomiting a deadly poison.
b. expelling its digestive system to entangle its attacker.
c. ejecting its bones to pierce its attacker.
d. releasing a sticky goo to suffocate its enemy.

Bubble Trouble:

A Denver, Colorado, company called Excuse Me, Inc., makes a soda called Rudy Begonia's Belcher that promises to deliver explosively loud belches after drinking it.

Seeing Red:

Ever wonder where the red coloring in lipstick and other cosmetics comes from? If the label says "natural colorings," chances are

that the red dye was made from beetle guts. The stuff is also used in fruit juice and other things we eat and drink. The cochineal beetle is found in Peru, where it lives on prickly pear cactus plants. While alive, the beetles are gray. But squash them and out squirts a rich, red liquid—perfect for giving the products we buy that bright red color that everybody likes. Hey, it's better than swallowing chemicals!

Yuck!

Researcher Buck Weimer of Pueblo, Colorado, spent several years perfecting . . .

a. Under-Ease—underwear with a filter to eliminate bad smells.
b. Sweet Gas—pills to make burps smell better.
c. Barf-a-Lot—deodorized barf bags for the airlines.
d. Arf!—perfumed pooper-scoopers.

The way the human body works is truly amazing. But some bodily functions are considered too impolite to talk about. See if you can pick out the fact below that is not only rude but totally false.

a. Once they get into the intestines, tapeworms can grow up to 30 feet long.
Believe It!   Not!

b. The word *rhinotillexomania* is the scientific name for compulsive nose picking.
Believe It!   Not!

c. People with lots of belly button lint have fewer upset stomachs.
Believe It!   Not!

d. Every day, the average person produces 1 quart of spit and 2.5 quarts of sweat.
Believe It!   Not!

BONUS QUESTION

The function of earwax is to . . .

a. keep people from hearing bad gossip about themselves.

b. trap nasty stuff like dirt and bugs.

c. clear up infections.

d. prevent loud noises from damaging eardrums.

You're walking along, minding your own business, and step in a pile of . . . you know. Pretty disgusting, right? Well, the stories you're about to read next give "disgusting" a whole new meaning!

Look Out Below! Ray Erickson of Santa Cruz, California, was enjoying a relaxing day on the water when a chunk of ice came crashing through the skylight of his boat. At first he couldn't figure out where it came from. But when the ice thawed, there was no mistaking what it was—toilet wastes that had been released by an airplane flying overhead!

Yuck!

Chemist Wayne Avellanet has invented a perfume that captures the smell of . . .

a. a frightened skunk.
b. rotting garbage.
c. a locker room.
d. a crowded subway.

37

Getting the Poop: In the spring of 2003, an infestation of caterpillars in Pontiac, Michigan, was so bad that residents could hear them crunching leaves, and pedestrians were forced to carry umbrellas to protect themselves from the tiny poop pellets raining down from the trees.

Pop Go the Crickets: "You drive down the street and they pop like Bubble Wrap," said Amy Nisbet of Elko, Nevada. She was describing the invasion of Mormon crickets that appeared out of the blue in June 2003 and covered almost every square inch of her town. The highways got so slippery after thousands of the 2.5-inch-long insects were squashed by cars that electronic overhead signs were programmed to alert motorists to slow down.

CRICKETS ON HIGHWAY
SLICK ROAD

82

The Collector: When neighbors called the Hong Kong police to complain about a disgusting smell, the officers found two apartments and two rooftop sheds filled with garbage—30 tons of it! The incredible mess of junk ran the gamut from broken umbrellas to discarded air conditioners to dead animals. Workers had to wear protective clothing to clear it away. Where was the person responsible for this huge mess? She was living under the stairway of the apartment building.

Stick Deodorant: Up until the 20th century, cities were extremely smelly places. That's because there were no flush toilets so people threw their bodily wastes into the streets. It smelled so bad that during the Elizabethan era, gentlemen in London carried walking sticks that released perfume into the air.

Slimed! In 1996, a train on the Casablanca-Fez railroad line in Morocco slipped off the rails after a horde of snails slimed the tracks.

Going Buggy: A swarm of bugs ravaged Nebraska in 1875. It was made up of an estimated 12.5 trillion locusts, weighing a total of 24.6 million tons. The creatures infested cities, towns, and fields alike, covering every square inch of the space they landed on. There were so many bugs crawling on the buildings that the buildings looked like they were moving!

Yuck!

In 1995, a group of students from the Minnesota New Country School in Le Sueur discovered . . .

a. a nearby pond filled with fish that had no tail fins.
b. a field of two-headed calves.
c. a flock of featherless birds.
d. hundreds of deformed frogs in a nearby pond.

The Molar Coaster: In 1991, workers in Blackpool, England, drained a lake near a roller coaster and found hundreds of sets of false teeth, several wigs, and six glass eyeballs.

Foul Fruit: Durian is a fruit the size of a football that grows in Southeast Asia. Its smell is so vile and overpowering that the fruit is banned from many hotels, restaurants, and even buses. A bus driver in Malaysia once stopped his bus to throw a passenger's durian out the window because the people seated nearby were throwing up!

Yuck!

Scientists in Nagoya, Japan, have determined that slime mold, which is a single-celled, brainless organism . . .

a. can change its shape and make its way through a maze to get food.
b. can multiply and strangle its victims.
c. is actually toad mucus.
d. is used as a lubricant in toothpaste.

Shoo, Fly: A plague of flies caused women to start using makeup in ancient Egypt. They used it not to beautify themselves, but as protection against the flies.

Bug Bonanza: In 1989, Peter Roman of Brooklyn, New York, won a prize of $1,000 in the World's Largest Roach contest with a cockroach that measured 1.88 inches long. Apparently, no one had an Australian burrowing cockroach. These little monsters can grow up to about 3 inches long!

Fish Fall: Over the years, all sorts of things have been sucked up by tornadoes or waterspouts and dropped miles away in driving rain. On August 6, 2000, residents of Norfolk, England, were pelted by a shower of dead fish! Pee-ew!

Frog Frenzy! It may not ever rain cats and dogs, but sometimes storms deliver more than mere rain, snow, or hail. History is full of reports of fish, jellyfish, snails, frogs, and even snakes falling from the sky. There's a written account of a storm of frogs that took place in about C.E. 200 in Macedonia, a region of ancient Greece. So many frogs fell on the roads, houses, and fields that people couldn't help but step on them as they escaped from the city. Squish!

Yuck!

Global warming is made much worse by . . .

a. large numbers of people bathing in the oceans.
b. sunbathers on the beach soaking up the sun's rays.
c. people burning candles at rock concerts.
d. the burps of cows and sheep.

Bad Tidings:

Now and then bathers are cautioned not to drink or swim in bodies of water that have suddenly turned red. The most likely cause for the discoloration is the appearance of water-borne organisms called dinoflagellates. These single-celled creatures release toxins in the water that leave fish bleeding and unable to swim. Scientists refer to these poisonous infestations as red tides.

Raining Maggots:

People racing yachts in the 1976 Olympic Games had an experience they hope will never be repeated. They were pelted by wriggling things falling from the sky during a storm. It didn't take them long to figure out that the rain was chock-full of live maggots! Another creepy storm like this was documented at least once before, when in 1968, a rain of thousands of maggots fell over Acapulco, Mexico.

Hiss-terical: For about ten years, the Alonsa School in Manitoba, Canada, became overcrowded every spring and fall—not with more students but with an infestation of garter snakes! The snakes were everywhere, crawling through cracks in the foundation, through the vents in the ceiling, and even among the books in the library. One unlucky 12th-grader took a book from a shelf and found a snake inside. The problem started when a snake den near the school was covered over. When the snakes came back in the fall, they found their old home was gone, so they set up housekeeping in the school. The snakes were harmless but unnerving. Luckily, the problem has gotten better since the completion of an artificial den near the school.

> ## Yuck!
>
> Titan arum is a flower that blooms in the jungle and smells like . . .
>
> **a.** rotting flesh.
> **b.** rotting garbage.
> **c.** human vomit.
> **d.** dog poop.

Brain Buster

Awful stuff doesn't only take place in the movies. Can you tell the three real-life events from the one that only happened in a horror movie?

a. Usually, residents of a neighborhood in Reading, Pennsylvania, woke up to the foul smell of a sewage plant. But one morning it was gone—replaced by the fragrance of a ton of garlic that was rotting in a nearby warehouse. Some of the residents thought the garlic was an improvement!

Believe It!   **Not!**

b. In 1954, radiation fallout from atomic bombs being tested in the desert created giant ants. Before they could be stopped, queen ants flew away and established a nest in the storm drains of Los Angeles, California. Luckily, the military was able to destroy the entire colony with machine guns and flamethrowers.

Believe It!   **Not!**

c. In Medieval times, instead of attacking a castle, an army might camp outside, preventing the defenders of the castle from getting fresh supplies of food. In an attempt to speed things up, the attackers sometimes hurled dead animals over the castle walls, hoping to spread disease.

Believe It!   **Not!**

d. In 1891, James Bartley, a 35-year-old seaman on the British whaler *Star of the East,* fell overboard and was swallowed by a sperm whale. The next day, the badly injured whale was found dead, floating on the surface. After hauling it aboard and slicing it open, the crew found Bartley, unconscious but still alive, in the whale's stomach.

Believe It!   **Not!**

• •

BONUS QUESTION

When customs inspectors at San Francisco International Airport opened a businessman's suitcase, they found . . .

a. several dead mice—lunch for the pet snake that was also in the bag.

b. a bag of buffalo manure, which is especially good fertilizer for flowers.

c. a rotting goat's head that the passenger was planning to have for lunch.

d. a dead guinea pig, a cherished pet the passenger wanted to bury in his own backyard.

Read this chapter and the next time your parents tell you to stop picking your nose because it's nasty, you can point out that there are a lot worse things you could be doing!

Yuck!

In the 1930s, the "Animal Woman" of Howe, Indiana, was known for her . . .

a. fear of bathing.
b. hairy body.
c. fanglike teeth.
d. habit of hunting and eating small animals—without cooking them.

Fat Attack!

Competitive eating is a popular pastime in the United States. According to the International Federation of Competitive Eating yearbook, Don "Moses" Lerman ate seven quarter-pound salted butter sticks in five minutes.

Body Snatchers:

In 1932, Robert Ripley visited the Paco Cemetery in Manila, Philippines. Here, corpses are placed in chambers in the cemetery's wall for an annual rental fee—but if families fail to pay the fee, the remains are taken away and burned.

Handy Tool:
A mummified hand, cut from the body of a hanged man, was carried by burglars in ancient England in the belief that it could open locked doors.

Pins and Needles:

B. A. Bryant of Waco, Texas, had a habit of sticking himself with pins and needles—as many as 100 at a time. He claimed he felt no pain while doing it, making one wonder exactly what he gained from it. Perhaps it was attention. Thousands watched him in amazement as he performed his feat at the Dallas Odditorium in 1937.

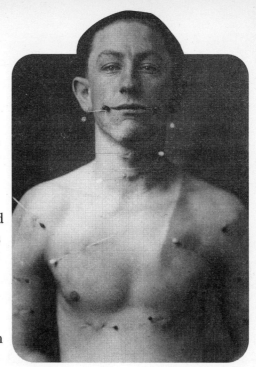

A Tisket, a Casket: People of the Torres Strait Islands place the heads of corpses on anthills until they are picked clean, then paint them red and display them in baskets.

Yuck!

To mourn the death of a relative, the Dani people of New Guinea have been known to . . .

a. shave off all their hair.
b. pull out a molar.
c. smear themselves with animal blood.
d. amputate a finger.

Tip Off: Malatian tribesmen of the Solomon Islands once advertised that they had killed and eaten many enemies by drilling holes in the tips of their own noses.

Land of the Living Dead: When the leader of the Dinka tribe in Sudan, Africa, becomes fatally ill or so old that death appears near, he is thrown into his grave—alive!

Flower Power: 'Abbad al-Mu'tadid, who ruled Seville, Spain, from 1042 to 1069, used the skulls of his enemies as planters for flowers.

Hands Off! Hanging on the Hospital of Rothenburg, Germany, since 1704 is a sign that warns: It is forbidden to quarrel, fight, or brawl here. Guilty parties will have their right hand chopped off.

Yuck!

Young men and women of Bali are initiated into adulthood by having their . . .

a. teeth filed.
b. heads shaved.
c. tongues pierced.
d. lips tattooed.

Beetlemania:

The ancient Egyptians worshiped a god called Khepera, which took the form of a man with a scarab beetle for a head. Khepera was a god of creation as well as an aspect of the sun god Ra. During the night, Khepera rolled the sun

from west to east through the underworld, ensuring it would rise again—or be reborn—the next morning. How did a beetle become a symbol of creation and rebirth? The scarab beetle is also called a dung beetle. It rolls dung into a ball and lays its eggs in it. When the eggs hatch, the larvae eat their way out and emerge from the dung fully grown. The ancient Egyptians, however, simply saw the young beetles as new life that had emerged, or been reborn, from dead matter.

Tomb Service: When the Sumerian Queen Shub-Ad of Ur died more than 4,000 years ago, 50 of her servants were killed and buried with her so that they could attend to her needs in the afterlife.

Fatheads:

In place of liquid perfumes, the ancient Egyptians wore large cones of scented fat on their heads that slowly melted and dribbled all over their bodies.

Watch Your Manners:

A 500-year-old book on etiquette urges diners not to grab their food with both hands and to use three fingers only.

Finger-Lickin' Good:

At the turn of the 19th century in Morocco, diners could only lick their fingers in strict order: little finger, middle finger, thumb, third finger, and index finger.

Ouch! At the annual Vegetarian Festival in Phuket, Thailand, participants skewer themselves instead of the food. During this nine-day festival, participants make ten commitments, which include eating no meat and drinking no alcohol. They spend the days in deep meditation, often entering trance states. At the height of the festival, helpers assist participants to puncture their cheeks with knives, skewers, broom handles, steel wire, and even spears. They feel the gods protect them from pain and, amazingly, there is little bleeding or scarring. Nevertheless, this is definitely *not* something you should try at home!

Yuck!

In the Middle Ages, a woman would present a man with an apple she'd held overnight in her armpit as a sign of . . .

a. extreme dislike.
b. annoyance.
c. affection.
d. gratitude.

Raw Deal: A young Banda woman is not considered ready for marriage until she has eaten an entire chicken— raw and without breaking any of its bones. Then she has to live an entire year without doing any work at all, not even feeding or bathing herself!

Body of Work: The practice of using body parts to create utilitarian objects can be unsettling to say the least. In Borneo, skulls were once used as money. And in South America, flutes used by Inca chieftains were made from the arm and leg bones of captured foes.

Who's for Dinner?

In 1552, Hans Staden, a German soldier who was shipwrecked off what is now Brazil, took refuge in a Portuguese coastal fort. He was later captured by the Tupinamba Indians. After his escape, he wrote a book that described how the Tupinamba often adopted captured prisoners, accepting them into their families and treating them with respect. According to Staden, there was just one catch—one day the prisoners would be killed and eaten.

What a Yolk! Forget about rice. During the Middle Ages, people at weddings showered the newlyweds with eggs!

Bloodthirsty: When they camped, Mongol armies would often drink the blood of their horses to sustain themselves. They did this so that they would not have to light a fire to cook food—a practice that would surely alert their enemies to their whereabouts.

Yuck!

Canadian jewelry designer Danny Pollack creates brooches out of . . .

a. used dentures.
b. dried fish guts.
c. goat intestines.
d. dead beetles.

Pharaoh Dust:
England's King Charles II (1630–1685) rubbed the dust collected from Egyptian mummies onto his skin in the belief that the greatness of the pharaohs would rub off on him.

Scent-sational! Not everyone tries to cover up body odor. Certain people in New Guinea have been known to stick their fingers in each other's armpits and rub the scent on themselves. That way they'll have a fragrant reminder of their loved ones long after they have left!

Marked Men:

As their initiation into adulthood, young men of the Shilluk people of Sudan, Africa, decorate their foreheads with beadlike marks, which are created by filling incisions with gunpowder.

In the Drink: To preserve their bodies so that they could be shipped home for burial, sailors who died in battle were often placed in vats of liquor. In 1805, when Admiral Horatio Nelson died in the Battle of Trafalgar, his body was placed in a barrel of brandy. Too bad the other sailors were not informed because they kept on tapping the barrel to have a drink!

Yuck!

Matthew Hopkins, the "witch-finder general" in 17th-century England, determined the guilt of a suspected witch by . . .

a. dropping her into a well to see if she floated.
b. setting her on fire to see if she would burn.
c. throwing her off a building to see if she could fly.
d. placing her in a vat of boiling oil to see if she could survive.

Baby Shower: Instead of saying, "Hi," the Masai people of East Africa spit at each other. Passing a friend without spitting is considered very bad manners. When a baby is born, everyone gathers around and showers it with spit, giving a new twist to the traditional baby shower of the West!

Yuck!

When an Asmat warrior of New Guinea dies, his eldest son inherits his . . .

a. shrunken head to display on a shrine in his home.
b. skull to use as a pillow at night.
c. teeth to string on a necklace.
d. embalmed heart to remember him by.

 Brain Buster

Some things may seem perfectly normal to the people who do them, while other people find them totally disgusting. Can you spot which of the practices below is grossly imaginative?

a. In Transylvania, young men present their fiancées with vials of their blood as tokens of their affection.

Believe It!   **Not!**

b. In South America, a game called Bimiti requires competitors to run along a track toward a trough of beer while bystanders throw handfuls of hot pepper and ashes at them.

Believe It!   **Not!**

c. In Coney Island, New York, Takeru "Tsunami" Kobayashi won the 88th Annual Nathan's Famous Hot Dog Eating Contest for the third straight year in 2003, downing 44.5 hot dogs in just 12 minutes.

Believe It!   **Not!**

d. In ancient Greece, women wore live bugs called cicadas leashed to golden threads as hair ornaments.

Believe It!   **Not!**

BONUS QUESTION

Queen Marguerite de Valois of Navarre, Spain, had pockets sewn into the lining of her voluminous hoopskirt so she could always carry with her . . .

a. pet bats whose wings had been clipped.

b. raw meat to feed her pet lions.

c. the embalmed hearts of her 34 sweethearts.

d. pet tarantulas to scare away a possible attacker.

CHAPTER 5 That's Sickening!

You may not like getting a shot or swallowing medicine when you don't feel well, but you'll soon find out you could have it a lot worse!

RIBBIT!

What a Leap!

An early folk remedy for whooping cough was to put a live frog in the patient's mouth. Natives of the *barrancas* (canyons) of Mexico's Sierra Madre Mountains treat headaches by stroking the patient's head with a live toad.

Yuck!

In ancient Germany, bald people who wanted to grow hair paid farmers to let . . .

a. cows lick their heads.
b. them roll in cow pies.
c. them sleep with the chickens.
d. them roll in the mud with pigs.

A Cut Above: It's no wonder the physicians of India were considered the best doctors in the ancient world. They got plenty of chances to practice their surgical skills on criminals who received punishments involving amputation! For internal surgery, such as removing kidney and bladder stones, they used black ants as clips instead of stitches. This practice might sound gross, but black ants give off an acid that helps prevent infection so patients would heal quickly.

Hand for an Eye: During the period between B.C.E. 1792 and 1750, doctors in Babylon had a lot to fear. There was a whole set of laws in the Code of Hammurabi that governed their behavior. For example, if a doctor treated an eye abscess and the patient went blind, the doctor's hand would be cut off as punishment.

Yuck!

The first antibiotic cream consisted of . . .

a. motor oil mixed with toothpaste.
b. carbolic acid mixed with linseed oil.
c. mouse ashes mixed with fish oil.
d. garlic mixed with ground seashells.

How Re-volt-ing!

In ancient Rome, shock treatments were used to treat headaches and joint pain. This treatment was used long before electricity was invented, so how were the shocks delivered? By torpedo rays. To cure headaches, the live fish was placed

against the patient's head, while joint pain was treated by having the patient stand on the fish in a pool of saltwater.

Kiss a Mouse, Cure a Cold: The Roman scholar Pliny the Elder (C.E. 23–79) believed that kissing a mouse was a surefire way to get rid of a cough.

COUGH! COUGH!

Peeping William:

In 1822, a Canadian hunter named Alexis St. Martin was accidentally shot in the stomach. When his wound healed, there was still a gaping hole in his side. But the doctor who treated him, Dr. William Beaumont, made the best of the botched surgery. He tied bits of food onto strings, then put them through the hole into St. Martin's stomach. Periodically, he'd pull the string out and examine the food. By this method, Beaumont learned the secrets of digestion and is credited for discovering that hydrochloric acid is part of the human digestive process. The experiments didn't seem to have harmed St. Martin, who lived for another 58 years!

Upper or Lower Berth:

In ancient Greece, people believed that a woman's womb had two compartments: one for girls and one for boys.

Yuck!

A common remedy for earaches in ancient Rome was . . .

a. a tea brewed with pigs' tails.
b. mouse ashes mixed with honey.
c. beetle juice tea.
d. ground firefly paste.

On Pins and Needles:

In 1927, a woman was rushed to the hospital with stomach pains. And no wonder! X-rays showed that she had been living on a very unhealthy diet. Inside her stomach were 2,533 objects—

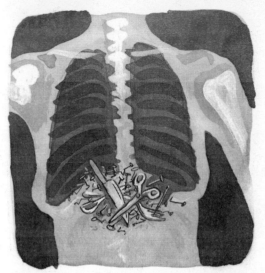

none of which was food! Doctors were astonished to count 947 bent pins among other assorted metal odds and ends.

Draining Experience: Long ago, starting in prehistoric times, bloodletting (piercing a vein so that the blood could pour out) became a common treatment for a variety of ailments—especially stomachaches. Why? Because people thought that illness was caused by too much blood. If bloodletting didn't work, there was always medicine made from ambergris, a substance that starts out in the intestines of the sperm whale. Once the smelly, black, gooey stuff is expelled, it hardens into pleasant-smelling, gray, waxy blobs that are found floating in the ocean or washed up on the shore.

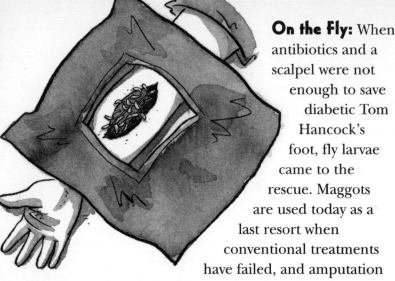

On the Fly: When antibiotics and a scalpel were not enough to save diabetic Tom Hancock's foot, fly larvae came to the rescue. Maggots are used today as a last resort when conventional treatments have failed, and amputation is the only alternative. The maggots, bred in a special lab, clean wounds by eating dead tissue and harmful bacteria. There's only one catch—they have to be removed within 72 hours or they'll turn into flies!

Say Ahh! One way to diagnose an illness is to examine the tongue. A red, furry tongue is a symptom of scarlet fever. A smooth, pale, shiny tongue might mean that the patient has pernicious anemia. A tongue covered with brown sores may indicate typhoid fever.

A Breath of Foul Air: In Indiana during the 19th century, a folk remedy for a head cold was to inhale the smell from a dirty sock nine times.

All Stuck Up: During the 19th century, doctors told their patients that if they chewed gum it would cause their intestines to stick together.

Yuck!

Every year, about 2,000 Japanese people become sick from . . .

a. drinking contaminated water.
b. smoking cigarettes contaminated with fecal matter.
c. swimming in lakes full of raw sewage.
d. eating raw fish infested with worms.

Getting an Earful: In France, an early treatment for deafness was to pour the blood of a mole into the patient's ear.

Sick to Death:

Thousands of people died in London during the great cholera epidemic of 1854. At that time it was thought that the disease was spread by evil strangers. But a local doctor, John Snow, didn't buy it. He discovered that among a group of healthy people working at a London brewery, one thing stood out—they did not drink from the Broad Street water pump. When Snow examined the water taken from the pump under a microscope, he found that it was filled with germs. From this, Snow deduced that cholera was caused by water that had been contaminated by London's open sewers.

Mummy Medicine: In
Europe during the 12th century, ancient Egyptian mummy skin with the wrappings still sticking to it was boiled and ground up for use as a medicine.

There's a Bug in My Tea: During the 1800s in Louisiana, a tea made with cockroaches was used as a remedy for tetanus, and cockroaches fried in oil with garlic were used to cure cases of indigestion.

Yuck!

In England, in the 1850s, a remedy for dysentery and epilepsy was to . . .

a. drink powdered human bones mixed with red wine.
b. swallow a few tablespoons of a syrup made with sheep's urine.
c. drink a glass of pureed jellyfish mixed with milk.
d. eat a plate of fried mice.

What Gall! In China, cow gallstones used in traditional herbal medicines sell for more than $7,000 a pound.

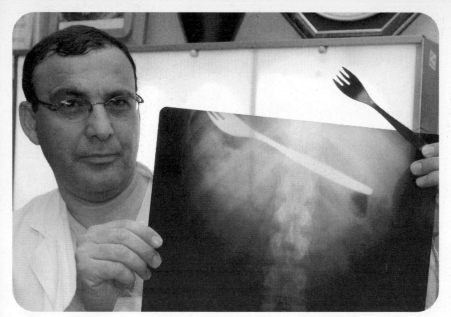

Roach In: An Israeli woman was cleaning her house when a cockroach flew into her mouth. When she tried to dislodge it, she ended up swallowing the fork she was using to pry it out from her throat. An X-ray showed that the fork was wedged sideways in her stomach. She had surgery to remove the fork—but the cockroach had already been digested.

For Crying Out Loud: Long ago, Persians used to save their tears in bottles because they were thought to have the special power to cure many illnesses.

Yuck!

Wart biters, used by Swedish peasants to get rid of warts, are . . .

a. toads.
b. caterpillars.
c. grasshopper-like insects.
d. lizards.

Here are some sickening facts and supergross tales straight from the Ripley's files. Can you find the one that's not only totally disgusting but totally untrue?

a. The Ancient Egyptians sometimes used urine to soften their skin—and urea is still used today in some hand creams and lotions.

Believe It!   Not!

b. While stuck in a traffic jam, Dr. Ira Kahn of Beirut, Lebanon, successfully performed surgery on himself to remove his inflamed appendix.

Believe It!   Not!

c. A four-year-old boy lived for four years with a family of dolphins. He was found by his uncle during a fishing trip, but the child was almost unrecognizable because he was suffering from barnacalitis, a condition in which the skin becomes covered with barnacles.

Believe It!   Not!

d. Two early treatments for skin diseases were to roll in the grass on the morning of St. John's Day and to eat a lizard.

Believe It!   Not!

BONUS QUESTION

In India, asthma was once thought to be cured by . . .

a. brushing a cat's tail across the bridge of the nose.

b. eating toadstools that grow in a graveyard.

c. inhaling the fumes from an open sewer.

d. swallowing live sardines smeared with secret herbs.

POP QUIZ

Are you totally grossed out yet? Hope not, because now you get to test your smarts about all the outrageous stuff you've just read in this book. Think you have all the answers? If you do, you can vastly improve your gross Brain Busters score!

1. Headcheese, a popular food in Europe, is actually . . .
a. lettuce boiled in milk and mixed with liver paté.
b. ground mushrooms and fiddlehead ferns.
c. pickled frogs' legs.
d. jellied lunch meat made from boiled animal heads.

2. Used to make dough stretchy, the additive 1-cysteine is derived from . . .
a. fingernails.
b. human hair.
c. yak hair.
d. fish bones.

3. At one time, a favorite meal of the Inuit was a dish made from the already digested contents of an animal's stomach.

Believe It!   **Not!**

4. Mucus sprayed by a sneeze can travel more than . . .
a. 60 miles per hour.
b. 30 miles per hour.
c. 10 miles per hour.
d. 100 miles per hour.

5. Nine-year-old Danny Denault won $500 in a contest for having . . .
a. the smelliest sneakers.
b. the most dandruff.
c. the worst body odor.
d. the worst-smelling breath.

6. A person's body odor can be a clue to his or her . . .
a. intelligence.
b. personality.
c. shoe size.
d. mood.

7. The red color in cosmetics often comes from a dye made from . . .
a. sheep's blood.
b. beetle guts.
c. red peppers.
d. ground salamander skin.

8. In the spring of 2003, people in Pontiac, Michigan, carried umbrellas to protect themselves from . . .

a. caterpillar poop.

b. pigeon droppings.

c. molting crickets.

d. airplane toilet wastes.

9. In 1991, workers in Blackpool, England, drained a lake near a roller coaster and found . . .

a. six mummies.

b. hundreds of dog skeletons.

c. a sunken roller coaster car filled with skeletons.

d. hundreds of false teeth, several wigs, and six glass eyeballs.

10. In C.E. 200 in Macedonia, an area of ancient Greece, there was a sudden storm that covered the city with dead fish.

Believe It!   **Not!**

11. The Malatian people of the Solomon Islands once advertised the fact that they'd killed and eaten many enemies by . . .

a. drilling holes in the tips of their own noses.

b. wearing necklaces made out of their enemies' teeth.

c. displaying their enemies' shrunken heads in curio cabinets.

d. wearing their enemies' shrunken heads on their belts.

12. At the annual Vegetarian Festival in Phuket, Thailand, participants . . .

a. eat so much rice that they vomit.

b. puncture their cheeks with knives, skewers, and other objects.

c. decorate their foreheads by making incisions in them and filling the holes with fava beans.

d. dress all in black and dance wildly through the streets.

13. The Masai people of Kenya greet newborn babies by spitting on them.

Believe It!   Not!

14. In Indiana during the 19th century, a folk remedy for a head cold was to . . .

a. eat boiled mouse brains.

b. drink the tears of a healthy family member.

c. chew dried pigs' ears.

d. inhale the smell from a dirty sock nine times.

15. An early remedy for whooping cough was to . . .

a. put a live frog in the patient's mouth.

b. kiss a mouse.

c. inhale moss from a graveyard at night.

d. wear a clove of garlic on a necklace.

Answer Key

Chapter 1
Bon Appétit
Page 5: **c.** worms.

Page 6: **b.** sago maggots.

Page 9: **d.** crickets.

Page 11: **a.** tadpoles.

Page 13: **c.** the beans taste better after they've been digested by a luak and separated from its poop.

Page 15: **b.** cattle dung.

Page 16: **b.** sea slugs.

Page 19: **d.** worms.

Page 20: **a.** another performer had soaked his red tights in.

Brain Buster: d. is false.

Bonus Question: a. seal flipper pie.

Chapter 2
Seriously Nasty
Page 23: **a.** enough dirt each day to cover seven floor tiles.

Page 25: **b.** food bits in vomit continue to be digested outside the body.

Page 27: **b.** an odor bomb that smells like vomit and human wastes.

Page 28: **c.** nine days.

Page 30: **c.** blew his tonsils out.

Page 33: **b.** expelling its digestive system to entangle its attacker.

Page 34: **a.** Under-Ease—underwear with a filter to eliminate bad smells.

Brain Buster: c. is false.

Bonus Question: b. trap nasty stuff like dirt and bugs.

Chapter 3
Most Foul

Page 37:   **d.** a crowded subway.

Page 39:   **d.** contains chemicals that can keep ice cream from thawing.

Page 41:   **d.** hundreds of deformed frogs in a nearby pond.

Page 42:   **a.** can change its shape and make its way through a maze to get food.

Page 44:   **d.** the burps of cows and sheep.

Page 46:   **a.** rotting flesh.

Brain Buster: b. is false.

Bonus Question: c. a rotting goat's head that the passenger was planning to have for lunch.

Chapter 4
Horrible Habits

Page 49:   **a.** fear of bathing.

Page 51:   **d.** amputate a finger.

Page 52:   **a.** teeth filed.

Page 55:   **c.** affection.

Page 57:   **a.** used dentures.

Page 59:   **a.** dropping her into a well to see if she floated.

Page 60:   **b.** skull to use as a pillow at night.

Brain Buster: a. is false.

Bonus Question: c. the embalmed hearts of her 34 sweethearts.

Chapter 5
That's Sickening!

Page 63:   **a.** cows lick their heads.

Page 64:   **b.** carbolic acid mixed with linseed oil.

Page 66:   **b.** mouse ashes mixed with honey.

Page 69:   **d.** eating raw fish infested with worms.

Page 71:   **a.** drink powdered human bones mixed with red wine.

Page 72:   **c.** grasshopper-like insects.

Brain Buster: **c.** is false.

Bonus Question: **d.** swallowing live sardines smeared with secret herbs.

Pop Quiz

1.   **d.**
2.   **b.**
3.   **Believe It!**
4.   **d.**
5.   **a.**
6.   **d.**
7.   **b.**
8.   **a.**
9.   **d.**
10.   **Not!**
11.   **a.**
12.   **b.**
13.   **Believe It!**
14.   **d.**
15.   **a.**

What's Your Ripley's Rank?

Ripley's Scorecard

Way to Go! You have just come into contact with some of the grossest stuff on the planet and you didn't get sick. What a trooper! When it comes to strong stomachs, you've proved that you're a real contender. Now it's time to rate your Ripley's knowledge. Are you a **Gross Groupie** or a **Yuck Master**? Add up your scores to find out!

Here's the scoring breakdown. Give yourself:
★ **10 points** for every **Yuck!** you answered correctly;
★ **20 points** for every fiction you spotted in the Ripley's Brain Busters;
★ **10 points** for every time you fielded a **Bonus Question**;
★ and **5 points** for every correct **Pop Quiz** question.

Here's a tally sheet:
Number of **Yuck!**
questions answered correctly: _____ x 10 = _____

Number of **Ripley's Brain Buster**
fictions spotted: _____ x 20 = _____

Number of **Bonus Questions**
you fielded: _____ x 10 = _____

Number of **Pop Quiz** questions
answered correctly: _____ x 5 = _____

Total the right column for your final score: _____

0-100
Sky-Scraper

When it comes to the gross and nasty side of life, you are head and shoulders above it all. Sure, you may not pay a lot of attention to the Yuck factor, but that's the way you like it. And while you totally get that the truth is often hard to swallow, you're not even going to try. Your friends may think you're squeamish, but you know that you just prefer not to think too much about the nasty stuff in life.

101-250
Gross Groupie

You enjoy a yucky story now and then as long as it doesn't involve worms, poop, or fish guts. And when it comes to sampling bug cuisine, you'll take a definite pass. Still, there's hope for you yet. After all, you did make it through this book, right?

251-400
Foul Player

There's not much that can gross you out. Baiting hooks, watching a gory operation, or even observing leeches suck blood during a medical procedure. You are one gross kid! An adventurous sort, you might even be tempted to sample a chocolate-coated bug or two!

401–575
Yuck Master

When it comes to gross stuff, you have the edge. You are down to earth, yet disgustingly savvy. Your mind is too bright to be turned off by anything gross, whether it's eating caterpillars or singing in the rain—of maggots. With your cast-iron stomach, you will scrape the bottom of the barrel, no matter how nasty, just as long as it will lead you to the truth.

Believe It!®

Photo Credits

Ripley Entertainment Inc. and the editors of this book wish to thank the following photographers, agents, and other individuals for permission to use and reprint the following photographs in this book. Any photographs included in this book that are not acknowledged below are property of the Ripley Archives. Great effort has been made to obtain permission from the owners of all materials included in this book. Any errors that may have been made are unintentional and will gladly be corrected in future printings if notice is sent to Ripley Entertainment Inc., 5728 Major Boulevard, Orlando, Florida 32819.

WE'D LOVE TO BELIEVE
YOU!

Do you have a Believe It or Not!
story that has happened to you or to someone
you know? If it's weird enough and if you would
like to share it, the people at Ripley's would love
to hear about it. You can send your
Believe It or Not! entries to:

The Director of the Archives
Ripley Entertainment Inc.
5728 Major Boulevard
Orlando, Florida 32819

Believe It!®